What are **YOU** looking at?

written and illustrated by
Katie O'Hara-Kelly

Sequoia Natural History Association

FIRST EDITION June 2000

ISBN 1-878441-11-6

$6.95

Printed in the United States

Written and illustrated by Katie O'Hara-Kelly

Published by the Sequoia Natural History Association
HCR 89, Box 10
Three Rivers, CA 93271
(559) 565-3759
http//:sequoiahistory.org

The non-profit Sequoia Natural History Association works in partnership with the National Park Service to provide educational publications and programs for Sequoia and Kings Canyon National Parks and Devils Postpile National Monument. All income of the Association is devoted to national park scientific and educational endeavors.

"What are **you** looking at, Ranger?"
asked the friendly young stranger.
"Would you mind if I took a peek?"

"Not at all," he replied.
"With your eyes open wide,
I think you'll find something unique!"

MULE DEER

As the winter turns to spring,
I'm looking at bright shades of green
below these snow filled peaks.

While I browse among the flowers,
songbirds sing from leafy towers
and snowmelt fills the creeks.

WESTERN TANAGER

We're looking for a place to rest,
before we start to build our nest
above the forest floor.

We've just flown for several weeks
over hills and mountain peaks,
2,000 miles or more!

STELLAR'S JAY

While I'm singing the "blues,"
through the campground I'll cruise
looking for something to eat.

I could eat a few bugs,
or some beetles and grubs,
but a pine nut would be quite a treat!

PLEASE!
DON'T FEED
THE ANIMALS

CHIPMUNK

I'm out looking for food,
because I'm in the mood,
for lots of scrumptious seeds.

Finding seeds is not a chore.
I find them on the forest floor
wherever my nose leads.

GIANT SEQUOIA TREE

I'm looking straight down,
300 feet to the ground,
at the people all looking at me.

As my branches all sway,
I can just hear them say,
"It's a Giant Sequoia Tree!"

BIG TREE TRAIL

TREE SQUIRREL

Way up in these branches
as autumn advances,
I'm looking for green cones to store.

With a thousand and one
my work's just begun.
Through winter I'll need a lot more!

BLACK BEAR

I'm looking at a lot of bugs,
beetles, ants, and big fat grubs,
inside this fallen tree!

I peeled off the rotten wood,
and found an insect neighborhood!
It's picnic time for me!

PILEATED WOODPECKER

I'm looking at an easy lunch,
the kinds of bugs I love to munch,
thanks to that Black Bear.

He has done the work for me,
by ripping up this rotten tree.
I wonder if he'll share?

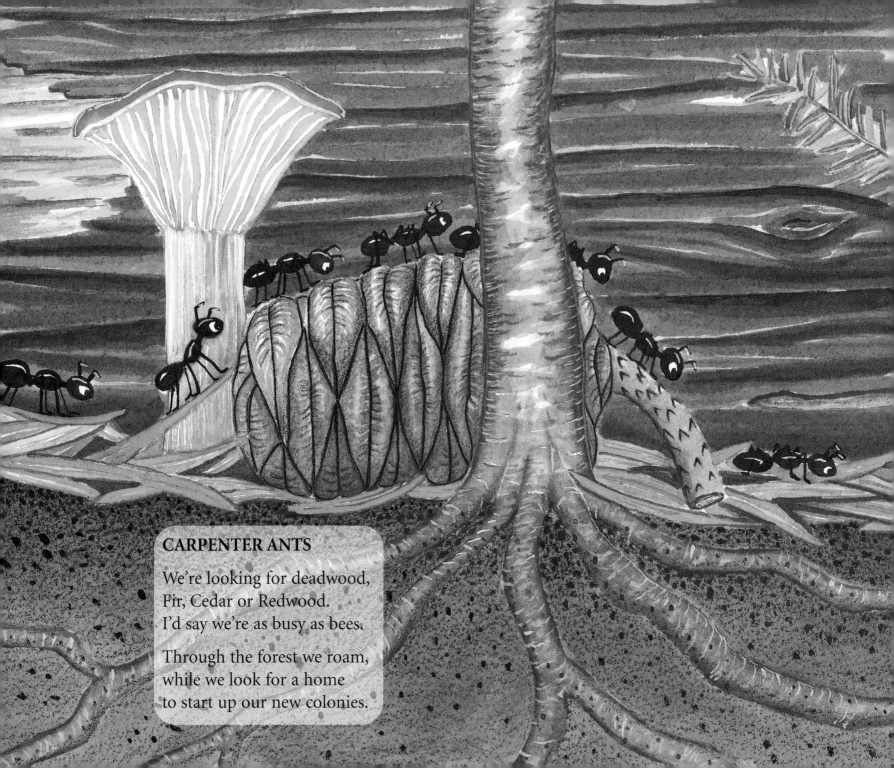

CARPENTER ANTS

We're looking for deadwood,
Fir, Cedar or Redwood.
I'd say we're as busy as bees.

Through the forest we roam,
while we look for a home
to start up our new colonies.

TRAPDOOR SPIDER

I'm watching and hoping
for some bug to come poking
around my hidden front door.

While I hide down in here,
they won't know that I'm near,
in my home on the forest floor!

POCKET GOPHER

I'm looking at some tender shoots,
and though my belly's full of roots,
I think I'll grab a bunch!

I'll stuff them in my empty cheeks,
then store them in my den for weeks.
The rest I'll eat for lunch!

RUBBER BOA

I'm looking for a place to rest,
and let my latest meal digest,
among these meadow flowers.

My next meal won't be too soon,
not before tomorrow noon,
or even 300 hours!

PACIFIC TREE FROG

While sunning on this fallen log,
I'm checking out an alpine bog.
There are insects in the air!

There're one or two I'd like to taste.
I'm feeling thin around my waist.
Oh Dragonflies beware!

DRAGONFLY

I'm looking with my giant eyes
at mosquitoes, gnats and damselflies.
They're hatching everywhere!

I've been zooming all around,
zooming up and zooming down,
to catch them in the air!

STONEFLY NYMPH

It's time to spread my wings and fly!
I'm looking for a place that's dry
out on this granite boulder.

As a nymph I lived in streams.
Soon I'll fly with brand new wings,
now that I've grown older.

AMERICAN DIPPER

I'm looking at a mountain stream,
that's clear and cold and glassy green.
I think I'll dive right in!

A bug or two would be a treat.
I wouldn't mind a bite to eat!
Let breakfast time begin!

TROUT

As I leap into the air,
I see insects everywhere!
I hope a few drop in!

Mayflies and mosquitos too,
would make a very tasty stew,
to start my morning swim!

MOSQUITO

I'm looking for a morning snack.
A hiker off the beaten track
is fishing over here!

He'll be hearing my wings beat
before the sun turns up the heat.
I'll "buzz" him in the ear!

ANNA'S HUMMINGBIRD

We're looking at peaks,
while we fill up our beaks
with nectar from alpine wildflowers.

As they sway in the breeze,
we will hover with bees,
and rest during cool thunder showers.

PIKA

Though it's late in the day
I'm still looking for hay.
I really should gather some more.

While the bears are asleep
and the snow is quite deep,
I'll snack on these underground stores!

GOLDEN EAGLE

I'm having some fun
out here in the sun,
looking at all of the peaks!

As I soar into view,
a marmot or two
let out some terrified squeaks!

YELLOW BELLIED MARMOT

I'm not fully awake,
from my snooze by the lake,
but an eagle's looking at me!

I'll just call an alarm,
to keep us from harm,
and then I will quickly flee!

SIERRA BIGHORN SHEEP

We're looking at the alpenglow
up here where the peaks have snow
throughout the summertime.

We climb along these cliffs so sheer,
because we're natural mountaineers
among these peaks alpine.

SIERRA NEVADA MOUNTAINS

We're looking at ewes
as we take in the views,
from up here at 12,000 feet!

We've been here for ages,
through geologic stages,
for endurance we can't be beat!

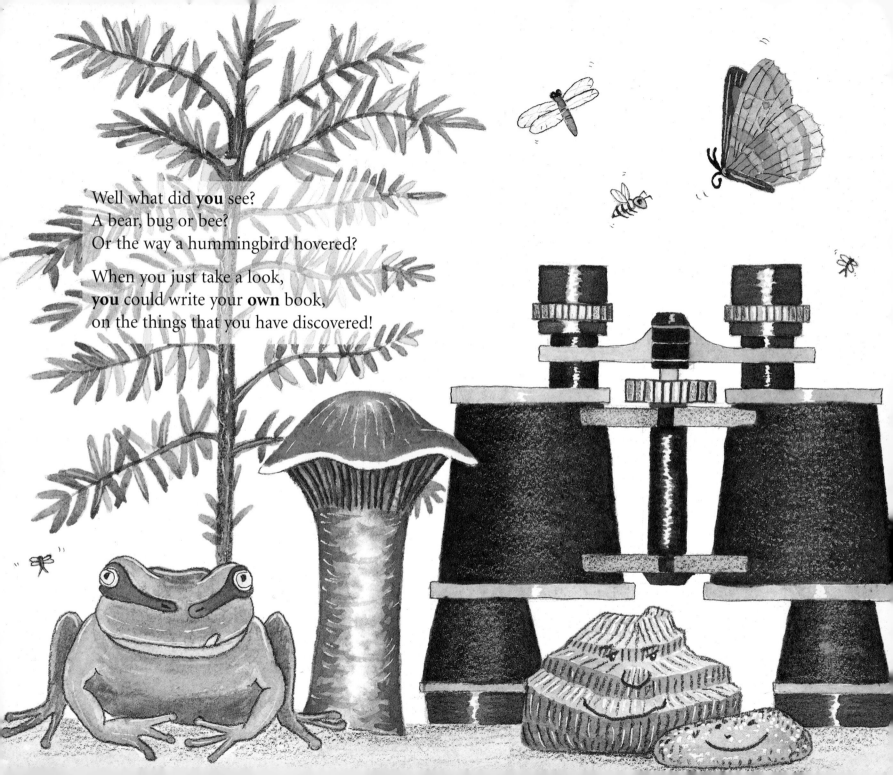

Well what did **you** see?
A bear, bug or bee?
Or the way a hummingbird hovered?

When you just take a look,
you could write your **own** book,
on the things that you have discovered!

NATURE NOTES

ACORN WOODPECKER

Acorn Woodpeckers are most commonly found in open oak woodlands in the foothills, but can also be found in mixed conifer forests where oaks are abundant. They live together in groups of three or more adults, in which all participate in the care and feeding of the young. They drill holes in the trunks of the trees and store acorns in them. A single tree may have more than 10,000 holes drilled in it!

ALLIGATOR LIZARD

Alligator Lizards eat insects, spiders and millipedes. They usually stay under protective covering, such as bushes, bark or rocks. They are slower than other lizards, and are easy to catch. However, they can give a good nip when handled!

AMERICAN DIPPER

American Dippers swim underwater, using their wings like fins! They can dive to the bottom of a creek, and walk around looking for aquatic insects! They oil their feathers to keep them waterproof. They have a special lens that covers their eyeball when under water. They close their nostrils when they dive, by contracting special muscles.

ANNA'S HUMMINGBIRD

Hummingbirds have the fastest wing beat of any bird, 70 beats per second! Hummingbirds can hover, fly forward and backwards! If it is lucky, a hummingbird may live for 10 years! Anna's Hummingbird is one of the most commonly seen species.

BLACK BEAR

Rotten logs are the favored habitat of many forest insects. Black Bears will rip open these logs to get at the insects inside! One Black Bear is known to have eaten 25,000 insects in one day! Black Bears also eat plants and occasionally feed on small rodents and carrion.

BLACK AND YELLOW GARDEN SPIDER

These brightly colored spiders are commonly found throughout North America. They weave flat circular webs in grasses, trees or bushes. The spider hangs head down at the web center or hides nearby.

CALIFORNIA SISTER

This butterfly feeds on flower nectar in the foothills and Yellow Pine forests.

CARPENTER ANTS

Carpenter Ants live in colonies. Their favored habitat is fallen logs. Carpenter Ants do not eat wood. They feed mainly on "honeydew," a clear watery liquid that aphids produce. Carpenter Ants excavate chambers in rotten logs, in which they live and raise their larvae. Small piles of sawdust, next to a rotten log, can indicate an active ant colony.

CHICKADEE

Chickadees are year round residents of the Sierran forests. They usually inhabit the middle to higher elevations, even during winter. They usually nest in abandoned woodpecker holes. They forage for insects in the foliage and bark of trees.

CHIPMUNK

Chipmunks store and eat the seeds of conifers and flowers, as well as the foliage of grasses, sedges, and shrubs. They store thousands of seeds in their burrows, as well as in shallow pits on the forest floor. They have a pair of internal cheek pouches, in which they carry their seeds.

COLUMBINE

Columbine grows in moist shaded areas, up to 8000' in elevation. Individual plants grow from 1.5' to 3.5' tall.

CORN LILY

Corn Lilies grow in damp meadows and stream banks, from 4500' to 11,000' in elevation. An individual plant may be 3' to 6' tall!

COW PARSNIP

Cow Parsnips grow 3' to 6' tall in moist meadows from middle elevations to 9000'.

DRAGONFLY

A dragonfly can see better than any other insect. Each big eye is made up of up to 28,000 tiny eyes! A dragonfly uses these big eyes to see moving insects. When flying, a dragonfly unfolds its legs into a basket-like net to catch insects in the air.

FIDDLENECK

The spiraled flower stalk of this wildflower resembles the spiraled wooden neck of a fiddle, hence the name "fiddleneck." They are usually found in the foothills, in grassy areas below 5,000'.

FIREWEED

Fireweed can rapidly take over burned or disturbed areas of northern forests, below

9,000' in elevation. However it is not restricted to those areas. An individual plant may be 1' to 7' tall!

GIANT SEQUOIA TREE

Most Giant Sequoias are 250' to 275' tall. They are the largest, by volume, of any living thing on earth. They can live to be 2,000 to 3,000 years old! The largest living tree on the earth is the General Sherman Tree, a Giant Sequoia in the Giant Forest Grove of Sequoia National Park.

LEOPARD LILY

Leopard Lilies form large colonies along stream banks and wet areas. They are generally found below 6000' in elevation. An individual plant can be 3' to 8' tall!

LONG HORNED BEETLE

There are a wide variety of Wood Boring Beetles that inhabit forests. Some species lay their eggs in bark crevices. Others will bore through the bark to lay their eggs. After hatching the larvae will live for years, chewing their way through the tree. The grooves you find on the heartwood of trees are the work of these larvae. After several years, the larvae will

pupate into winged adults. These adults will bore their way to the surface of the tree and fly away. The beetle pictured in this book is an adult and larvae of the Long Horned Beetle.

MOSQUITO

The mosquito in your ear is probably a female! Female mosquitoes are the only ones that bite! Male mosquitoes feed on nectar, while females feed mainly on blood. The females need protein rich blood to produce their eggs. In a season, females will lay thousands of eggs in pools and moist areas. That whining buzz is the sound of their wings beating at an amazing 400 to 600 beats per second!

MULE DEER

Mule Deer migrate up to higher elevations, as spring returns to the mountains. At the onset of winter, Mule Deer will migrate down from higher elevations to the foothills. Lack of forage and deep snow cause this migration. Mule Deer constantly travel even while in the foothills. They browse in small groups or loose herds while traveling. They forage mainly in the morning, late afternoon, and evening. During the daytime they bed down in secluded areas.

MUSHROOM

Mushrooms are a type of fungi. They are one of the main visible decomposers on the forest floor. They reproduce with spores, rather than seeds, and do not have flowers. The main part of the mushroom is underground, in the form of fine hair-like filaments, called mycelium.

PACIFIC TREE FROG

Pacific Tree Frogs can be found in wet or damp environments at any elevation in the Sierra. Despite their name, they do not live in trees. The males will sing at any time of the year, day or night. The females do not sing. They have sticky toe pads, which help them climb. They feed on insects, which they catch with their long sticky tongues.

PIKA

Pikas usually live above 7,000' on rocky talus slopes. They do not hibernate during winter, but sleep and eat in their underground burrows. They spend much of the summer and early fall gathering and storing vegetation. The vegetation is stacked and dried in the sun, before it is stored underground. This activity is called "haying."

PILEATED WOODPECKER

Pileated Woodpeckers are the largest woodpeckers in the Sierra Nevada, 16" to 19" in length! They chisel out large holes in tree trunks, while searching for wood boring beetles, carpenter ants, and larvae. They have a long, barb-tipped tongue which is recessed back along the top of their skulls. This tongue is used to extract insects from hard to reach places!

POCKET GOPHER

Pocket Gophers do most of their foraging for plants in their underground tunnels. Occasionally, they will venture out at dusk, to forage a few feet from their burrow. Owls, coyotes, foxes, weasels, bobcats, and snakes prey on Pocket Gophers. They dig mazes of burrows, can run backwards, and will even plug up their burrow entrances to avoid being eaten.

RED TAILED HAWK

Red Tailed Hawks, and all birds of prey, have the best vision of any animal. They can spot a mouse from 3,000' in the air! A person on the ground couldn't even see a hawk that far away. They eat squirrels, gophers, mice, snakes, and lizards, but not marmots. Marmots are too big for hawks.

REIN ORCHID

Rein Orchids are found along wet stream banks and seeps. They are found up to 11,000' in elevation. They reproduce annually from underground tubers.

RUBBER BOA

Rubber Boas prey on small mammals, lizards, and baby birds. Like all Boas they are constrictors. They quickly wrap themselves around their prey and squeeze them until they stop moving. Depending on the size of a meal, they may not eat again for several weeks to a month. Rubber Boas are often found under rocks and logs near streams or wet meadows.

SCARLET MONKEY FLOWER

Scarlet Monkey Flower is also called Cardinal Flower, due to its bright red color. They grow along stream banks and moist areas below 8,000' in elevation.

SEEP SPRING MONKEY FLOWER

Monkey Flowers come in a wide variety of species. Seep Spring Monkey Flowers are common along streams and moist places, from the coast to the mountains.

SHOOTING STAR

Shooting Stars are in the Primrose Family. They grow in wet areas from 2,300' to 10,000' in elevation.

SIERRA BIGHORN SHEEP

The Sierra Bighorn Sheep are extremely rare. They avoid humans and inhabit the high peaks of the Sierra Nevada in summer and fall. They spend the day resting and browsing in alpine meadows. The males have large curving horns. The females have goat-like spikes. In winter, they migrate down to the desert on the eastern slope of the Sierra.

SIERRA NEVADA MOUNTAINS

The Sierra Nevada Mountain Range is about 450 miles long and 60 to 80 miles wide. It is considered to be one continuous block of granite! About 10 million years ago this block began to rise on the east and dip down on the west. Glacial activity began about 3 million years ago, resulting in the formation of "U" shaped valleys and rock moraines. Mount Whitney, located on the east side of the Sierras, is the highest peak in the contiguous United States, at 14,495'!

SKY PILOT

Sky Pilot is found only on dry rocky ridges and slopes at 10,000' to 14,000' in elevation. It has adapted itself to higher climates by being short and having numerous hairy leaves.

STELLAR'S JAY

Please don't feed wild animals! It is better for them to forage for their own natural foods. Stellar's Jays normally eat seeds, nuts, insects, fruit, small mammals, as well as the eggs and young of small birds! Unfortunately in campgrounds, they have learned to eat human garbage and handouts. They are loud and noisy in the campground, but quiet and secretive around their nest sites. In fact, they are one of the most secretive nesters in the Sierra Nevada!

STONEFLY NYMPH

Stonefly Nymphs are one of the many aquatic insects that inhabit mountain streams. They can be found in highly oxygenated water, clinging to submerged rocks. They feed on algae, bacteria, and dead plant detritus. They have hair-like gills, hooked feet, and two tail filaments. Although they look fierce, they do not bite when handled. After 1 to 3 years, they crawl out of the stream to begin their adult life. When their outer skin dries, it splits open along the middle of their back. They emerge from this old skin, dry out and fly away. As adults they only live long enough to mate and lay eggs, usually 1 to 2 weeks.

TRAPDOOR SPIDER

Trapdoor Spiders live in underground tunnels on the forest floor. Instead of spinning a web, this spider uses its silk to line the walls and door of its tunnel. The door is camouflaged with dead pine/fir needles and twigs on top, and is hinged from the inside. When a Trapdoor Spider feels the vibrations of some small critter walking by, it will rush out of its tunnel and capture its prey!

TREE SQUIRREL

Tree Squirrels, as their name implies, live in trees! They nest in abandoned woodpecker holes, or in nests they construct out of branches and leaves. They remain active all yearw and do not hibernate. In fall they may stockpile thousands of green cones for winter forage. There are several types of Tree Squirrels, including Western Grey, Douglas, and the Northern Flying Squirrel.

RAINBOW TROUT

Rainbow Trout live in clear, cool, oxygenated water. They feed on aquatic insects and their larvae, as well as terrestrial insects that fall into the water. Mayflies and mosquitoes have aquatic larval stages, and adult terrestrial forms. Mosquito larvae are found in ponds and lakes, just under the surface of the water. Mayfly larvae inhabit the rocky beds of streams and rivers.

WESTERN TANAGER

Western Tanagers spend their winter in Southern Mexico and Central America. Some migrate to the Sierra Nevada in spring, reaching the foothills in April/May. As spring advances, they move up to the coniferous forests to nest. They build cup shaped nests on horizontal branches, 5' to 50' above the forest floor. The males are bright yellow with a red head, black back, and black wings. The females are yellow with black wings and a greenish back. Their return migration begins in October.

YELLOW BELLIED MARMOT

During the day, Yellow Bellied Marmots can be seen resting on large warm rocks that command a wide view. When one is threatened by danger, it will sound an alarm whistle and run for its burrow. Their burrows can be found underneath the boulders of large talus slopes. Throughout spring, summer, and fall, Yellow Bellied Marmots gorge on alpine vegetation. They are quite fat by the time winter comes around! During winter they are in hibernation, living off this stored body fat.